The HCG Diet for Beginners: Lose Weight Quickly and Healthy with the HCG Diet - A Complete Guide Including Tips, Recipes, Meal Plans

Table of Contents

Understanding HCG Lifestyle Benefits

There are those that wake up at 4 or 5 am to get ahead of the schedule. We all know at least one of those people. The women look great in their size 5 or 6 dress clothes or workout clothes. The men could take of their shirt and never be ashamed. They carry on about how good they feel due to this 'new lifestyle etc." Often times in our minds we envy them, but we put on a smile, and listen to them talk about this new diet. But the fact of the matter is we can look as happy, healthy and glow just as much as they do. Sometimes the frustrations of failed diets can make us envious or just down right... mean and not want to be around these fun SKINNY people. But there is light at the end of the tunnel. This is the one stop for all the HCG information you are ever going to need.

The thing we DON'T always listen to... is that is ENTIRELY MANAGEABLE for us (you) to look and feel this way as well. Clears the mind, offers realistic health checkups, and overall, is affordable and easy to do. So what is this 'miracle lifestyle'? It is known as the HCG diet, and yes, it is a lifestyle. Something that you can do. Something that is affordable, manageable and something the WHOLE family can benefits from. Here you will learn about the benefits, the meal plans, recipes and overall effects of the HCG diet.

What the heck is *HCG?*

This is the part when many people tune out, you start throwing out big words and medical terms and descriptions. But the bottom line is you should know what you're putting into your body and what you're doing to it. So, follow along the best you can, at the end you will know what this is all about. There are several different sites out there that information on HCG. But you will get a little from this site, a little form that site. Well, I don't know about you but I hate having to go to several different websites to get information on ONE dang topic. Here you are going to get all the information you need. The tools to choose right form of HCG, How to build a great grocery list (sample attached) and overall, how to make some really great meals from a small section of foods. (Since this is a 500-800 calorie diet, you do need to get creative from time to time). Not to mention you will know what HCG means. Once you are done reading this guide you will be ready to start working out, eating healthy and if you have a family, you will be just as eager to share this information with them as your friends are to share theirs with you!

HCG: Human Chorionic Gonadotropin. This is generally produced when a woman is pregnant. But it does have other purposes as well. This is a natural hormone that is produced by your body as a defense or protector of your metabolism. This is the result of your brain and your body.

Simple terms: this is a secretion of the body because your brain is telling your body it is CRUCIAL to burn fats within your bod to keep it clean and healthy. It offers the potential to burin up to 3500-4000 calories per day, which can result in up to 2-5 pounds off per day.

HCG Tips
Many people don't realize this is a diet that will require hormone injections, which was described above. But you are also on a restricted diet of 500 calories per day (remember you are trying to lose weight after all). But we have also put together a few tips for you in case you want to take a more proactive approach to your diet.

1. Vitamins and Nutrition- when you are on a restricted diet such as this it's important that you are still getting the appropriate amount of nutrients. So, taking a multi-vitamin daily is the best way to ensure the daily nutrients needed.
2. Hydration- Obviously drinking plenty of water (no empty calories) or tea is going to be as important as drinking water. It is important to make sure you drink 8-10+ glasses of water per day. And make sure that each glass is 8 full ounces.
3. Fitness- Get in a good 20 minute cardio workout daily
4. Diet- Meal plans are available.
5. Supplements- You can add different supplement drops to your water. This falls under that multivitamin category as well.
6. Retrain your brain- No emotional eating or eating from boredom...Retrain your brain
7. Fiber- Again this is something that is very important.

FAQ on the HCG Diet

Now anytime someone looks into changing their diet, sleep patterns and overall lifestyle there are going to be questions. At least there SHOULD be questions. Here we have collaborated a collection of frequently asked questions regarding the low calorie diet. You will learn about the different types of HCG, how to shop, what to shop for and last but not least, again, here are some of the most commonly asked questions regarding the diet.

Would my doctor recommend it?

Seeing as how the HCG diet is NOT YET FDA approved chances are you doctor would not openly invite you to start this low calorie diet. But not too many doctors will tell you NOT to convert to the diet unless you have some underlying health condition. But it would be wise to consult with a doctor or nutritionist as you dive into the new lifestyle. There are several ways to lose weight and live healthy. This is one that is controversial, but it is effective.

500-800 calories per day *really?*

As many people STOP reading when they see they are only able to consume 500 calories per day; I'm going to say, keep reading. You may be hungry a few days into the diet. But tell me what diet doesn't expect you to cut BACK on your food intake. So while your body and mine adjust to the new diet, you may be slightly hungry for a few days. But your mind and body will readjust and the hunger will subside.

I heard this is dangerous... What are the side effects?

Every diet or lifestyle change comes with a list of side effects and dangers. But so do prescription medications. Yes you are injecting hormones into your body to burn calories. There will be dangers and side effects and that is why it is CRUCIAL to stay under the care of your family physician. We have put together a standard list of side effects.

- Rapid weight loss can cause kidney issues such as stones and gallstones
- Headache
- Fatigue
- Irritability and mood swings

- Depression
- Fluid Retention
- Blood clots
- Ovarian cysts
- Testicular tumors

Fitness & Nutrition

It is important to integrate any fitness program into your new lifestyle. Regardless of what diet you are looking into. Here we have put together just a few different fitness suggestions and programs for you to choose from. There is no one size fits all diet or weight loss program. So it is important to find one that works best for you hence another great reason to have a trustworthy physician and or nutritionist on board to oversee your new diet and lifestyle.

- 30 minutes of Cardio daily
- 60 minutes Zumba daily
- Running/Jogging daily
- Weight Training

Which one is for you?

The HCG diet has been around for some time now, but a lot of people don't realize that there is more than one way to use HCG. There are drops and injections. Here we have gathered information on all of the current HCG options. You will see that some of them cost more than others; some are new and some involve injections. It all boils down to which you are most comfortable with, what you can afford and of course, which your doctor feels is best for you.

Drops

Currently, this is one of the most common forms of the HCG diet. Probably because it is the least painful of the three forms. But more so, because it is the cheapest form of the HCG that is currently out there.

Pellets

This is the newest form of HCG that is out there. Because this is so new, there are not a whole lot of reviews or information out there currently. This is new so you have to remember that there is not a lot of research on the pellets. You can either try them and take your chances or wait for more reviews to come out.

Injections

This was how it all got started. The injections were clearly developed or other reasons. Medical reasons. For those needing hormone replacements, help with pregnancy and other medically necessary reasons. This has also become the most DANGEROUS of methods for the HCG diet. But it is still very popular.

Sprays

This is fairly new as well, but the bottom line is the growing trend for the HCG diet. Something that has proven to be more than a trend. There are a few different kinds of sprays. Which include oral, nasal and sublingual.

When you are looking at the different ways to use the HCG It is very important that you adhere to the warnings, know the difference between 'knock off' brands and don't purchase fraudulent products. The bottom line is they are out there. Often times they are brought in from Mexico and other countries and are not made legally and will not always contain he proper (and safe) ingredients.

HCG Diet & Nutrition

Rather than hear about all the things you CAN'T eat with the HCG diet and lifestyle sometimes it is better to concentrate on the things you CAN eat, and different ways to cook them. Here we have put together a rough outline of some of the different items you can use to make different dishes.

Proteins

There are two meals you are able to add proteins to your diet. For both lunch and dinner you are able to have 100 grams (which is about 3 ½ ounces) per serving. Which means you can have chicken, lean cuts of beef and sirloin (roast). For special occasions you can have shrimp, lobster or white fish. Of course you will want to cut any and all fats from the meats and you can broil or grill them.

Non-starch

Of course vegetable are going to be a huge part of your HCG diet. This will become your main source of fiber which is awesome for your digestive system. You will want to transition over to iceberg lettuce, green leaf, and Boston lettuce for your greens. Spinach, beets, and cabbage. A few other vegetables you will be able to have are: fennel, celery, radishes, asparagus and cucumbers.

In between snacks

It is going to be important that you eat snacks when you can. This is something that a lot of people forget, or think isn't 'allowed' but with the HCG diet, it is ok to eat, you just need to watch the calories. So no snacking on "empty calorie snacks". Grab an apple, orange, some grapes, or strawberries. It is important to fuel your body so snacks are allowed. Another thing that people forget. You may have a 'limited resource' of allowed foods, but you have endless limits on flavor. It is truly ok to use all kinds of different seasonings, rubs, marinades etc. These are all things that you can use to spice up your diet (quite literally). Nothing has to taste the same twice if you don't want it to.

The other thing that is really important is that you always carry something to drink with you. Water is going to become your new best friend. And as a companion you can squeeze a lemon, lime or orange into your water for added flavor. All three well help 'curb' your appetite as well. When you are looking at hot drinks you can have hot tea and a little coffee. Always use artificial sweeteners

Things to keep in mind about your new Lifestyle

Now that you have all the information on the HCG diet. Who to talk to, the different forms of HCG and what you need to talk to your doctor about, and so on. Than it is all on you to go and make the changes. We can offer you the information, hand you the work out options, recipes, and food items and last but not least encourage you to see your doctor and ask them to follow you. But last but not least we want to offer you a few more works of encouragement and advice as you start the first day of your new HEALTHY life.

Final tips:

- Remember it is ok to use things such as mustard powder, garlic powder vinegar and basil and any other type of seasoning.
- Fruits and SOME carbs are ok for in between meal snacks but not for MEALTIME
- DRINK AND STAY HYDRATED. Remember to add lemon or something flavorful but natural to keep you hydrated and help you stay full longer

Sample Grocery List for HCG dieter

- Green tea
- Unfiltered Apple cider vinegar
- Extra virgin olive oil Vitamin enriched Vegetable oil
- Chicken and Beef Broth
- Iceberg lettuce
- Broccoli
- Cucumbers
- Lemons
- Strawberries
- Tomatoes
- Wheat thins
- Salsa
- Seasonings (different varieties)
- Chicken (white meat)
- Shrimp and other seafood's

- Lean Roast
- 93% lean ground beef
- Lean steak

Now remember this is just a fresh start for you. But as I mentioned before, this is something that can be taught, something that you now have all the tools for and overall, it is in your control. How you choose to live the rest of your life. Take the time to experiment with the different foods and seasonings. Find what you enjoy, and what maybe isn't for you. Make different meal plans.

Start out weekly than as you familiarize yourself with the new diet you can expand to monthly and so on. It is all about the workout plan, the diet and the HCG injections/drops/sprays. What is so great about this diet is that it may not be a "one size fits all diet" but it is possible to create the perfect diet and lifestyle for yourself through the HCG diet. Take what you have learned here and share it with others. As we talked about in the beginning, you will have all the tools you need to live a healthy and happier lifestyle. Remember the key to great meals is experimenting with different seasonings, marinades and other forms of flavoring without having to add unhealthy foods to your diet.

The first step to your new lifestyle is complete. You sought out the information, took the time to read this, and now it's time for you to make that doctors appointment. Get the clean bill of health, talk to them about your new goals and diet. From here on you are in control of your diet, your health and your life.

The HCG Basics: Phase 1 Diet

With each of the different phases, there are going to be specific things you can and shouldn't eat. So here you are going to get a little breakdown as to what the Phase 1 diet is all about and what things you can (and should) eat while you are stocking up on carbs etc. When they say this is your loading phase that is almost an underestimate. A lot of time people think that since it's a diet, they should take that term 'loading days' with a grain of salt and just... Not overdo it (Which, don't get us wrong we don't want you stuffing your face until you puke). So we put this together to help you understand the phase 1 diet a little better.

In most cases the loading days will consist of two days where you will stock up on foods that are high in fat. Now as easy as that sounds, there is a catch. What you need to keep in mind is you do need to avoid foods that are high in sugar. Now that is suggested by Dr. Simeons, but if you have a few things here and there, don't worry, it will be ok. So, as easy as it would be to just load up on sugar based foods, it really isn't the best option. Here we have added a few of the foods that can help you through the phase 1 diet:

- Bacon, sausage, Canadian bacon
- White Bread with peanut butter and jelly
- Eggs
- Fried pork chops, Fried chicken, Fried beef steak
- Condiments
- Chocolate
- Pastries with cream sugar or whipped icing

Now obviously some of the foods we mentioned here are sugar based, but again we didn't say you *couldn't* eat them, we just said they may not be the best option for your phase 1 diet. When you get started you need to wake up, weigh yourself, use your HCG drops, then you can begin eating. When you do this both days you will be off to the right start with your new HCG diet. When you are still a little unsure about the phase 1 diet, there are several recipes that are available to you here as well. Just keep in mind that after these first 2 days of loading you are going to start your 500 calorie diet, which these calories that you take in now are going to help keep your body going and help your metabolism work overtime while you are transitioning into your next phase.

Phase One: Sample Menu Plan

As you start your journey with the HCG diet, it is going to be important that you eat the right foods for each phase. Here we have put together a *sample* meal plan for the loading days (which are the first two days of phase 1. This is the startup before you go into phase 2 where you will begin your 500 calorie intake. The sample phase 1 meal plan below is just that a sample, you can substitute different foods from the below if they aren't your cup of tea. Just remember that this is your time to stock up. Be sure to take your HCG as recommended as well.

Menu plane phase 1:

Wake up, Breakfast meal: ½ C oatmeal with almonds and fresh berries

Mid-morning snack: Slice of bread with peanut butter and banana

Lunch: ½ roast beef sandwich with condiments (mayo, mustard or your preference) with chips and yogurt.

Mid-afternoon snack: 1 C potato Salad and bagel with cream cheese

Supper: Grilled chicken, sliced and sautéed onion over fettuccini with fresh fruit

Before bed snack: Sliced apples and sliced bananas with almond butter or peanut butter, cup of hot tea

Now, you have the loading stage for two days. That is what phase 1 is about, stocking up on the carbs and protein before you begin the lower calorie intake. You can take the menu above and mix it up with other foods, or you can eat what you want as you want, but if you *don't* follow this 2 day loading stage, you will NOT see the weight come off as quickly as you would if you followed the guidelines. It is really important that you don't cheat on the diet, or read articles about 'Hcg cheats" you will hear about how it worked, and so on, but this not true. You will not lose the weight properly if you don't follow each step.

This is just one menu plan. There are other recipes available throughout the site, and you will be able to go through and come up with your own menu plan as well. Also as you go through and follow each phase you will be able to find recipes, menu plans and information about each phase throughout this site. If you have questions refer to the main page talking about Phase 1. Here you will get basic information about the diet, and phase one of the HCG diet.

Phase 1 Recipes

Throughout the book you have learned about each of phases, there are recipes, information about HCG, each of the meal plans for the diet and more. Here you will are going to get recipes and information about the HCG phase 1 diet recipes. There are a few more recipes for you to try during your loading days, and they can be modified to work throughout your diet as well. If you find that you're not interested in the diets below, you can modify them. That is one of the great things about phase 1. This is your loading stage where you can indulge in cravings and eat what you like. Go ahead and try one of the recipes below, you may surprise yourself. Here we put together some *ideas* for phase 1 diet recipes. You can create your own loading recipes from these morning breakfasts.

It is important that you that breakfast is one of the most important meals of the day. Especially when you are stocking up through this first stage.

1. Eggs and scallions- When you make your eggs it is important that you eat the entire egg, not just egg whites. You can add a little flaxseed to your eggs and scallions as well. Or you can do eggs and sausage through phase one as well.
2. Oats- this is your typical oatmeal in the morning. A full cup on oatmeal sprinkled with some cinnamon, and cut up your favorite fruit to add with your oatmeal.
3. Yogurt- Not the low fat stuff, you will have the chance to eat nonfat yogurt later in the diet as well. A cup of yogurt and a banana, this with an English muffin with butter almond butter
4. Cream cheese bagel, fresh fruit and cottage cheese (again NOT the low fat version)
5. Sliced tomatoes, scrambled egg and 2 slices of toast with your favorite spread
6. Egg omelet made with coconut oil, ham, sausage and few bell peppers and onion diced up inside the omelet with your favorite juice or coffee (black)
7. Bowl of cereal with 1 C whole milk, a slice of cantaloupe, and ½ bagel
8. Whole bagel with cream cheese, slice of watermelon, 1 glass of whole milk

9. 1 biscuit ½ C gravy with sausage, 1 C orange juice heavy pulp and ½ C grapes
10. English muffin toasted with favorite jam, 2 eggs over easy, with favorite piece of fruit

Starting with phase one can seem line the easy phase. This is where you get to eat what you want, when you want in order to stock up for the 500 calorie diet that you will be starting in the phase 2. Now many times people think that is going to be the easy portion, but we forget most foods we crave contain sugar. Now we aren't saying you can't have sugar, we are saying eat in moderation and concentrate on other carbs such as bread, pasta, dressings etc. Here we have put together a short compilation of recipes for phase 1. You can modify these to taste.

Rosemary Steak

Ingredients:

- Steak or your choice
- 1 T rice vinegar
- 1 T dried rosemary
- 3 Garlic cloves, minced
- ½ tsp crushed red pepper
- Baked potato

Directions: Start with marinating your steak with the ingredients above and let soak on both sides for about 15 minutes each, then you can grill to your desire. Serve with a baked potato with all the toppings.

Noodles and Greens

Ingredients:

- 1 T vegetable oil
- 1 12 oz. smoked ham
- ½ onion cut up
- 8 garlic cloves, diced
- 2 bay leaves
- ¼ C red wine vinegar
- 2 T hot pepper sauce
- 5 C chicken broth
- 2 bags mustard greens
- 1 bag egg noodles
- 6 slices bacon cooked and cut up
- Salt and pepper to taste

Directions: In skillet cook ham and then add onions, garlic and bay leaves. Add remaining ingredients slowly one at a time, stirring as they cook on low in skillet. Make noodles in separate sauce pan. Serve ham mixture over noodles.

Coconut Nut Rice

Ingredients:

- 2 C uncooked black rice
- 2 ½ C water
- 1 12 oz. can coconut milk
- 1 tsp sugar
- 1 tsp coconut oil
- 1 shallot, diced
- ½ C macadamia nuts, smashed
- 3 T Coconut

Directions: Start with water, milk, sugar over heat until sugar dissolves, stir in rice and boil. Simmer for 30-45 minutes, remove and let stand. Separate pan add oil, shallots and salt to taste for about 3-4 minutes over low heat. Add shallots, nuts and coconut to rice and serve.

These are just *three* recipes of hundreds that are out there for your loading stage. When you are looking for different recipes that help load up you can look for recipes that are for athletes, or 'before marathon' recipes. These will be stocked with carbs and nutrients that your body needs to prepare for phase 2.

Phase 2 Diet Recipes

Summertime Chili

Ingredients

- 100 g 93% lean ground beef
- ½ tomato diced
- 1 tsp minced garlic
- Red pepper Seasoning
- 2 C water

Directions: Beef ground beef, drain grease and add garlic, and stir well. Next you want to add remaining ingredients and boil. Reduce heat and let simmer. Single Serving, for each person double recipe for more servings. Count yours out first for your phase 1 meal.

Seafood Tomatoes

Ingredients:

- 1 Tablespoon fresh Basil
- 2 tsp parsley, chopped
- 1 large tomato cut, cored and emptied
- 1 tsp lemon juice
- ½ C spinach

Directions: Wash the empty tomato bases with water and spray with pam. Season with salt and pepper to taste. Place tomatoes on cookie sheet, or on foil for your grill. Heat over grill until tomatoes are blacked (not softened). DO NOT BURN THEM. Sautee your shrimp over skillet on medium heat, add garlic and other seasonings Make sure they are cooked thoroughly and dip shrimp in lemon juice for taste. Then you will stuff the tomatoes with the shrimp and spinach. This is one serving, you will need the above ingredients per serving.

Phase 1 Salad Dressing

Ingredients

- 1 Tablespoon lemon juice
- ½ Tablespoon Liquid Amino
- ½ Tablespoon white vinegar
- 1 t. sesame oil
- 1 t. soy sauce
- 1 t. fresh ginger

Directions: This is rather simple and it is great for phase 1 salads, mix all ingredients together and you can serve on any salad.

Beef & Broccoli

Ingredients:

- I large Shallot
- 1 tsp minced garlic
- 1 ½ tsp caraway seeds
- 2 tsp paprika smoke
- 1 T. apple cider vinegar
- 2 C beef stock
- 1 lb beef Steak
- Salt and pepper to taste

Directions: you want to start with your meat, you can cook this in a slow cooker, all day on slow for 6-8 hours or you can cook this on your stove. Once meat is cooked bring your shallots and garlic to a skillet and brown. Drip a little vinegar as you go. Add beef stock and simmer for 10 minutes. Add your beef steak cut into bit size pieces to your garlic and beef stock. Serves 4-6

Zesty Chicken Sandwich

Ingredients

- One Yellow Onion, diced
- 1 sliced orange
- Lemon juice
- 1 lbs. chicken tenderloins
- Poultry Herbs
- Minced Garlic for flavor

Directions: This is a crockpot meal, which is always wonderful. What you are going to do is orange all the fruit and vegetables in the bottom of the crockpot first then add your seasonings followed by the tenderloins. Add ½ C water and cook for 4-6 hours on low. Serves 7-8

Beef Salad

Ingredients:

- 1 lbs. Beef
- 1 Dill pickle
- 1 tomato
- 1 ½ C Shredded lettuce
- 1 tsp mustard

Directions: One of the rather simple salads, you prepare your lettuce, tomato and pickle at your preference, cook beef in skillet until brown and mix in mustard. Pour beef over salad and serve.

Apple Chicken with Kale noodles

Ingredients:

- 100g Boneless Skinless Breast
- 1 tsp Extra virgin oil
- 1 Crisp Apple
- 2 C Kale- washed and shredded
- 1 tbs. Sliced Shallot

Directions: Go through and season your chicken first, and you will grill chicken until done. Bowl 2 Qtr. water and boil, add oil, garlic until soft. Add remaining ingredients and continue stirring. Serve chicken as main dish and everything in pan over the chicken. Serves 1-2

Tikki-Tacos

Ingredients:

- Lettuce
- Shredded Chicken Breasts
- Spinach
- Onions- Cut up
- Jalapeños
- Salsa
- Taco Seasoning
- Lime Juice
- Minced Garlic
- Cilantro

Directions: these are made just as most tacos. Shred and cook you chicken in a skillet, once cooked add ½ C water with taco seasoning to chicken and let simmer; in a separate small skillet, add diced onions, spinach, jalapeños, and the salsa, simmer than add remaining ingredients. Once all heated and mixed add chicken to tortilla shell, and add desired amount of mixing. Serves 6-8/

Phase 2 Apple Delicious Pie

Ingredients:

- 1 Granny Apple, Diced
- 1 Tbsp. Ground Cinnamon
- Lemon juice

Directions: Slice apples to desired size, you can use a small single serve dish or you can add one apple per serving. Layer apples with cinnamon then place dish in microwave for 2 ½ minutes. Enjoy.

Shrimp Cocktail Salad and Sauce

Ingredients:

- 1 lbs. Large shrimp
- 2 T. Old Bay Seasoning
- Shredded romaine
- Lemon Juice
- 1 tsp. cilantro
- Homemade cocktail sauce

Directions: Boil medium pot of water, add salt, and seasoning then the shrimp. Add lettuce and make the salads from the ingredients, then drain the shrimp and set on top of the salad.

Phase 4 Recipes

Coconut Meat

Ingredients:

- 1-2 lbs. ground chicken breast
- 1 bag croutons
- ¼ C milk
- 1 Egg
- ½ T Oregano
- 1/2 C coconut flakes
- ½ t dry minced onion

Directions: Start with the milk in a bowl large enough to put toast into, let soak. Mix remaining ingredients together. This should form just over a dozen round balls. Bake at 400 degrees in oven for about 15 minutes.

Thee apple a day

Ingredients:

- 1 medium to large apple; sliced
- ½ C nonfat cottage cheese
- Cinnamon
- 1 Truvia packet

Directions: If you are starting with a sliced apple, and in a separate bowl mix cinnamon and the Truvia, into the cottage cheese. You will use the dip you have just made to dip your sliced apples into. You can also take the cinnamon and sprinkle it over the apple slices beforehand as well.

Cool Cucumber Salad

Ingredients:

- 1 Sliced and diced cucumber
- 1 tomato sliced to preference
- ¼ C sliced green onions
- 1 tsp lemon (squeeze fresh juice)
- ½ tsp minced garlic
- 4 oz. can white meat of your preference (chicken or tuna)

Directions: Add all the ingredients in a bowl, and toss salad. You can add allowed HCG virgin olive oil if you want.

The Chicken Noodle cold cure

Ingredients:

- 1 can diced chicken
- Diced celery
- 1 ½ C chicken broth
- ½ tsp minced garlic
- 1 tsp dry onion flakes
- Salt and pepper to taste

Directions: Start with a medium size saucepan and heat over low to medium and add your broth, and remaining ingredients one at a time, and bring soup to a boil, then remove from heat to not burn, then simmer for 10-15 minutes. Serve.

HCG Winter Steak

Ingredients:

- 1 lb filet, strip or rib eye
- 1 tsp mustard powder
- 2 tsp vinegar
- Salt and pepper to taste
- 1 tsp minced garlic

Directions: Start by mixing all the ingredients together, and coat steak with spices and start grill. You can grill this over high heat on 5-7 minutes each side. Serve.

T.G.I.M (Thank Goodness it's Monday) Coffee

Ingredients:

- Fresh Black coffee
- Splenda to taste
- Cinnamon
- Ice

Directions: If you have a mixer, you just simply put all the ingredients in the mixer, blend until ice is crushed, pour into glass, and drink!

Rabbits Lunch

Ingredients:

- 1 lb deli sliced turkey
- ¼ C honey mustard
- ½ C mozzarella cheese (shredded)
- 1 piece lettuce or spinach per wrap

Directions: open your flour tortilla and spread money mustard over shell and lay remaining ingredients over shell, wrap and heat for 25-30 seconds until cheese melts. Serve with carrot sticks or cucumbers.

HCG BBQ Sauce

Ingredients:

- Diced Turkey Bacon
- Minced Onion
- Diced onion
- 1 small can tomato paste
- 1 can diet cola of your preference
- ¼ C ketchup
- 3T mustard
- 1 T Worchester sauce
- ½ C water
- 2 T Hot Sauce

Directions: Brown meat and shred. Add onion and brown and stir in garlic, then add remaining ingredients, stir and simmer for roughly 30-40 minutes, while stirring so it doesn't stick to the bottom of the pan. Serve.

Sparkle POP Cake

Ingredients:

- Yellow cake mix
- Diet Sprite can
- Orange Jell-O

Directions: Make the cake according to the directions on the box but add the can of Diet Sprite. In a separate pan, mix Jell-O and boiling water, per the directions of the box. Pour into cake pan. Chill for about 30 -45 minutes. Great with ice cream or Cool Whip toppings.

Pork Pot Luck

Ingredients:

- 2 lbs. pork tenderloin
- 12 oz. Sauerkraut
- Hot sauce or mustard
- 1 C diet Soda

Directions: Prepare meat, cut fat etc. and lay ingredients in crock pot and set for 8 hours on low to medium.

38936808R00028

Made in the USA
San Bernardino, CA
15 September 2016